TEACHER EDITION

MW01690424

REAL-WORLD CHEMISTRY

PROJECTS

McGraw Hill Glencoe

The McGraw·Hill Companies

Glencoe

Send all inquiries to:
Glencoe/McGraw-Hill
8787 Orion Place
Columbus, OH 43240-4027

ISBN: 978-0-07-891230-6
MHID: 0-07-891230-X

Printed in the United States of America.

6 7 8 9 10 QVS 15 14 13

Table of Contents

To the Teacher

Real-World Chemistry provides hands-on activities and projects that relate chemistry to students' everyday lives. This supplement encourages students to go beyond the classroom to investigate the chemistry behind the products and processes that are part of their world. From batteries to cosmetics, from cooking to energy production, students will gain a greater appreciation for the applications of chemistry.

Real-World Chemistry contains projects for each chapter of the textbook. Background information introduces students to the topic. The projects that follow vary between experiments, simple activities, surveys, and research. For all projects, students are encouraged to go out into the community, capitalizing on the immense human resources that bring chemistry to life.

Name ______________________ Date ____________ Class ____________

CHAPTER 1

Alloys: When Mixtures Are Better Than Pure Substances

Background

With more than 80 known metallic elements, you might assume that there is one for every possible application. But that isn't the case. For example, aircraft manufacturers would like to have a metal that is very strong, withstands the high temperatures of jet engines, does not corrode, and is lightweight. No naturally occurring metal meets all these requirements perfectly. But chemists and metallurgists have invented mixtures of metals, called alloys, that meet these requirements better than natural metals.

Research

Today, hundreds of different alloys exist, all invented to meet some special industrial, commercial, residential, or research need. A number of the most commonly used alloys are listed in the table on page 2. See if you can discover one or more ways in which each of these alloys is used in your home or community. Begin by exploring products in your home that contain metal to see if any contain one or more of the alloys listed. Then visit a local hardware store and examine some of the metallic products sold there. See which of the listed alloys you can find and determine how each is used. Finally, when you have completed your research, find a textbook or a chemical reference handbook that includes information on alloys. In the spaces provided in the table, list the composition and uses of each of the given alloys.

Activity

Alloys are important in our world because of the special physical properties they possess. For example, some alloys are very resistant to corrosion and rust, others conduct an electrical current well, and still others melt at low temperatures. This activity will introduce you to some of the interesting physical properties of certain alloys.

Your teacher will provide you with samples of different alloys. In addition, you can try to find examples of alloys in your own home to add to this selection. Write down the names of the alloys in the first column of the chart below.

Examine each of the alloys in order to determine the properties listed in columns 2 – 6 in the table. The term *luster* refers to the alloy's appearance. Use terms such as "shiny," "grainy," "tough," and "dull." You can find the density of each alloy by following these directions.

1. Find the mass of one piece of the first alloy. Record that number in column 4.
2. Fill a 100-mL graduated cylinder to the 50.0 mL mark with tap water.
3. Add the alloy to the graduated cylinder and read the new level of water in the cylinder.
4. Subtract the volume of the water before adding the alloy from the volume of water *after* adding the alloy (50.0 mL). This is the volume of the alloy piece. Record this value in column 5 of the table.
5. Find the density of the alloy by dividing its mass by its volume. Record this number in column 6 of the table.
6. Repeat this procedure with each alloy sample.

Name ______________________ Date ____________ Class ____________

CHAPTER 1

Some Common Alloys: Their Compositions		
Alloy	**Composition (percent by mass)**	**Use**
Dental amalgam		
Cast iron		
Coinage metal		
Electronic solder		
Monel		
Nichrome		
Pewter		
Type metal		
Wood's metal		

Finally, suggest a possible use for any one of the alloys you studied for this activity.

Name of Alloy	Color	Luster	Mass of Sample	Volume of Sample	Density

Name _______________ Date _______ Class _______

CHAPTER 2

Cathode Ray Tubes

Background

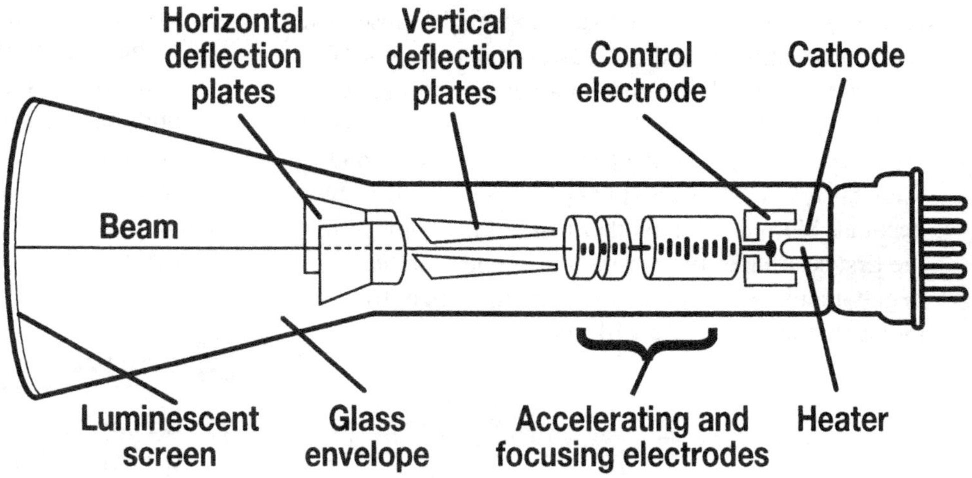

J.J. Thomson used a cathode ray tube (CRT) to discover the electron; different kinds of cathode ray tubes have important applications. Computer monitors and television picture tubes are two of the most familiar, although the use of CRTs in these industries is decreasing. A cathode ray tube generates a beam of electrons. When you look at a computer monitor or a television set that uses a CRT display, you see the beam of electrons striking the back of the screen. Here is how the cathode ray tube in a television picture tube works.

Electrons are generated by heating a piece of metal, the cathode, to a high temperature, usually about 825°C. Cesium metal is commonly used in making the cathode. A positively charged piece of metal, the anode, attracts the electrons. They move from the cathode to the anode and some pass through a hole in the middle of the anode.

Recall that J.J. Thomsom studied an electron beam by deflecting it with magnets or electrically charged plates. The same principle is used to keep the electrons traveling in a sharp, narrow beam. The beam of electrons is focused by a magnetic or an electric field, much the way light is focused by a lens. The electrons travel toward a screen covered with a thin layer of a phosphor, a substance that gives off light when struck by electrons. A commonly used phosphor is zinc sulfide, which gives off a greenish glow when struck by electrons.

The image on the screen is "painted" as magnetic and electrical fields deflect the beam, directing it toward an upper corner of the display screen and then moving it back and forth across the screen, from top to bottom. An electron beam typically scans the entire display screen about 60 times every second.

The picture tube for a color television set may contain three electron guns, one for each of the primary colors: red, green, and blue. The video signal that enters the tube is divided into three parts, one part for each of the three colors. The signal also carries information about the relative intensity of each color. A picture of the sky would contain an intense blue component and relatively little of green and red. A white object would require all three colors at high intensity.

The electron beams transmitted by the electron guns have no color. The color comes from the particular phosphor struck by each beam. One phosphor, yttrium silicate, produces a purplish-blue glow; zinc orthosilicate, a yellowish-green glow; yttrium oxide, a reddish glow; and zinc cadmium sulfide, a bluish glow.

CHAPTER 2

Another important property of phosphors is persistence, the time it takes them to fade after being struck by an electron beam. In a color television set, the glow produced by a phosphor has to last long enough to register on the eye, but not so long that it appears in subsequent scans. Remember that the screen is scanned about 60 times per second. If the phosphor continues to glow too long after being struck by the electron beam, the color will remain from the first scan after the second scan has begun. When that happens, the overall picture becomes blurred. On the other hand, if the color from the first scan fades out before the second scan has begun, there will be a blank spot on the screen for a moment, and the picture will flutter.

Activity

You can find out more details about television picture tubes from two sources. First, you can visit a television repair store and talk with a technician. Perhaps she or he will show you some of the parts that go into a television tube and the functions of each part. Second, you can read more about television picture tubes in encyclopedias or dictionaries of technology, college chemistry or physics textbooks, books about cathode ray tubes or television reception, or internet sources.

Report

Summarize what you have learned by making a colored diagram of a television picture tube. The diagram should contain enough detail so that an observer can see how the tube works, but not so much detail that it gets confusing. Show your diagram to a friend, relative, or neighbor who is unfamiliar with cathode ray tubes to see if he or she understands the ideas you are trying to illustrate.

Name _______________ Date _______________ Class _______________

CHAPTER 3

Keeping Swimming Pools Clean

Background

One property that the halogens, the elements that make up Group 17 of the periodic table, have in common is that they kill disease-causing microorganisms. You are probably familiar with the use of iodine as an antiseptic, a substance used to cleanse wounds. You may also know that chlorine is used to prevent the growth of algae and bacteria in swimming pools. Compounds of chlorine, such as hypochlorous acid (HClO), have the same effect as chlorine.

In some large pools, chlorine gas is added directly to water to kill harmful microorganisms. In other cases, a compound of chlorine is added to the water. For example, the "liquid chlorine" used to purify swimming pools is actually a solution containing the compound sodium hypochlorite. When sodium hypochlorite is added to water, it reacts with water to form hypochlorous acid, a compound that kills algae and bacteria.

Anyone who owns a pool should maintain a regular schedule of chlorinating the pool water. Businesses such as motels and hotels, which have pools open to the public, are required to maintain such schedules and to keep careful records of the chlorine level in their pools. In this activity, you will learn how pools are chlorinated and then tested for chlorine levels.

CHAPTER 3

Part One

Visit any public swimming pool in your area. It could be a city pool, a school pool, or a pool at a hotel. Ask the manager to have someone show you how the pool is chlorinated and how chlorination tests are carried out. Then, answer these questions.

1. In what form is chlorine added to the pool?
2. How often is the pool chlorinated?
3. What tests does the city, county, or state require to be done on the swimming pool water?
4. What tests other than those for chlorine levels are required?

Part Two

Visit the local public health official that is responsible for licensing swimming pools in your town, city, or county. Ask the official these questions.

1. What are the required levels of chlorine in pools? Why are those levels chosen?
2. How are other pool tests, if any, related to the amount of chlorine present in a pool?
3. Does the public health department favor one form of water purification in pools over another? Why or why not?
4. How carefully do pool managers appear to follow county rules about chlorination? What does the county do when pools are not maintained properly?

Part Three

During your interviews in Part One or Part Two, or by referring to a chemistry textbook, discover the answers to the following questions.

1. What chemical reaction(s) occurs when chlorine gas is added to water?
2. Describe what changes occur when sodium hypochlorite or calcium hypochlorite is added to water.
3. What chemical reaction(s) is used to test for the presence of chlorine in pool water?

Conclusions

Summarize the results of your research by writing a one-page report that explains how the water in swimming pools is purified by chlorination and how to test for chlorine levels. The report should be short, complete, and easy for the average nonscientist consumer to read.

Name ______________________ Date ______________ Class ______________

CHAPTER 4

How Noble, Those Gases!

Background

Because noble gases are essentially unreactive, they sometimes get very little instruction time in introductory chemistry classes. However, these gases have some important applications in daily life. In fact, most of the applications are possible just because the gases are unreactive.

For example, xenon is used in the manufacture of lamps designed to produce light that is similar to daylight. Such lamps can produce intense and brilliant light that can be seen through fog. Krypton is also used in light bulbs, both incandescent and fluorescent. In incandescent bulbs, it provides an inert atmosphere around the filament, helping to make the filament last longer. In fluorescent bulbs, it produces a bluish color that can be used in signs.

Research

The applications just mentioned reflect only a few of the many ways in which the noble gases are used in everyday life and in research. Find information on other applications of this interesting chemical family. To begin, look in your telephone directory for the names of companies in your area that sell compressed gases. Arrange for a visit to one or more of these companies. Bring along the school video camera to record what you learn. Talk with the owners or managers and ask them to tell you about the ways in which the gases they sell are used in your community. Your school or community library will also be a good source of information on the uses of the noble gases, as will the Internet.

A nearby college or university could be another good resource. Try to locate a teacher at such an institution who knows about the uses of the noble gases. Arrange for an interview with that person to find out more about this family of elements. Your local hospital is another place that uses and has information about the noble gases. Some of the gases are used for diagnosing and treating medical problems. Try to contact someone at the hospital who can talk with you about this subject.

Report

Compile the results of your research in a table that summarizes the ways in which the noble gases are used in your community. Try to find at least five important uses each for helium, neon, and argon; and at least two important uses each for krypton, xenon, and radon. If possible, construct a table that will be interesting and attractive for other members of the class and the general public. Use photographs, videos, or samples of materials that demonstrate the uses of the noble gases.

Name ______________________ Date ____________ Class ____________

CHAPTER 5

What's in a name?

Background

Chemical compounds can have some strange-sounding and fairly complicated names. How do they get these complicated names?

As you already know, many compounds have two names. For example, the compound with the formula HgS is correctly called mercury(II) sulfide. But mercury(II) sulfide is also known by the common name cinnabar.

Names are longer and the process of naming can be more complex when describing organic compounds, such as those used as drugs and medicines. For example, you probably do not recognize the name N-cyano-N´-methyl-N´-[2-[[(5-methyl-1H-imidazol-4-yl)methyl]thio]ethyl] guanidine. Yet, for many years, this compound was the most frequently prescribed medication in the world. It is a drug used to treat stomach acidity and prevent the formation of ulcers.

Many compounds with very complicated names, like this one, are often given simpler names that doctors, pharmacists, and other health-care workers can refer to more easily. These names are known as generic names. The generic name for the compound described in the previous paragraph is cimetidine.

Drugs customarily have yet another name, the brand name. Each manufacturer gives a brand name to the form of the generic drug that it makes. For example, cimetidine is sold in drug stores under at least two dozen brand names, including Acibilin, Acinil, Cimal, Cimetag, Cimetum, Edalene, Dyspamet, Gastromet, Metracin, Peptol, Tagamet, and Ulcimet.

Research

For this project, find out the names of chemicals in your own home. Do a search of your kitchen cabinets, workroom shelves, bathroom cabinets, and other places where household chemicals might be found. Write down the name of every product you find and the first chemical listed on the product's label. Refer to a handbook of chemistry or a drug handbook to find the scientific name of any drugs or other chemicals you list.

Report

Combine the results of your research with those of other students in class. On the blackboard or a large sheet of butcher paper, make a chart like the small chart in the example shown on the next page, or use the large chart provided. Write the names of all the household chemicals you found in the proper columns, keeping all the brand names for any one chemical together, as shown in the small chart on the next page.

Name ______________________ Date ____________ Class ____________

CHAPTER 5

Examples:

Scientific Name	Common Name	Generic Name	Brand Name
N-(4-hydroxyphenyl)-acetamide		acetaminophen	Eneril; Panadol; Tylenol; Valadol
magnesium hydroxide	milk of magnesia		Maalox; Mylanta; Di-Gel

Scientific Name	Common Name	Generic Name	Brand Name

Name ______________________ Date ____________ Class ____________

CHAPTER 6

Photographic Development and Blueprints

Background

You have learned that heat can change the rate at which chemical reactions take place. Another form of energy that can have a similar effect is light. Some chemical changes take place very slowly or not at all unless they are exposed to light. The chemical changes that take place in photography are examples of such reactions.

Film used for black-and-white photography consists of a thin layer of gelatin on top of a clear plastic sheet. Embedded within the gelatin are tiny grains of silver bromide, AgBr. When silver bromide crystals are exposed to light, a series of complex chemical reactions occurs. Some of the colorless silver ions (Ag^+) are converted to black silver atoms (Ag). The more light that strikes an area of the photographic film, the larger is the number of silver ions that are converted to silver atoms, and the darker the area becomes.

The process of converting exposed silver ions to silver atoms is completed by adding a developer to the exposed film. The developer is a chemical such as hydroquinone, $C_6H_4(OH)_2$. A developer guarantees that any silver ions that have been exposed to light are actually converted to silver atoms.

The final step in developing an exposed film is to remove unexposed silver bromide from the gelatin. This step is accomplished with a fixer, a chemical that reacts with silver bromide and produces substances that can easily be washed out of the gelatin. A common fixer is the chemical known as sodium thiosulfate ($Na_2S_2O_3$), also known as "hypo."

Part One

Find someone who has experience developing film, and ask him or her to demonstrate the process to you. Make a note of the chemicals that are used in the developing process and ask the photographer what function each chemical plays. You may wish to refer to a college chemistry text for more information on the function of each chemical.

Part Two

See what you can find out about the process of color photography. The person you spoke with for Part One may be able to help you. Or, you can consult books that discuss the process. You may want to work with one or two other students to find out what chemical changes take place in the taking and development of a color photograph.

Part Three

Blueprint paper is made using chemicals that respond to light energy. Here are the steps to follow in making a piece of blueprint paper. The solutions you need must be prepared in a darkroom or other place where there is little light. The first solution consists of 10 g of potassium ferricyanide, $K_3Fe(CN)_6$, dissolved in 50 mL of water. The second solution contains 10 g of iron(III) ammonium citrate, $Fe(NH_4)_3(C_6H_5O_7)_2$, dissolved in 50 mL of water. Keep both solutions in the dark until you are ready to use them.

To make the blueprint paper, thoroughly mix equal amounts of the two solutions in a shallow tray in a darkroom. Then dip one side of a sheet of white paper into the mixture a few times and hang it up to dry. Do not let light shine onto the paper at any time.

When the paper has thoroughly dried, you can use it to make a blueprint. Place the sheet of blueprint paper, greenish side up, on a piece of window glass. Place an object, such as a leaf, on top of the blueprint paper. Then place a second piece of window glass on top of the object. Expose this setup to light for anywhere from 30 seconds to 3 minutes. Remove the blueprint paper, wash it thoroughly in a pan of water, and place it on a flat surface to dry.

Conclusions

Summarize the results of your research by preparing a poster that shows the steps involved in taking and developing a black-and-white photograph or a color photograph. You can also display the blueprint that you made. Wherever possible, write chemical equations that describe the chemical changes that take place in each step of the photography process and in the making and using of blueprints.

Name ______________________ Date ____________ Class ____________

CHAPTER 7

Lighting the Dark

Background

The invention of artificial lighting systems thousands of years ago transformed human civilization. Instead of restricting their activities to daylight hours, humans could remain active as late into the night as they wanted. And they could explore areas of darkness, such as caves, with the aid of their artificial lights.

At first, artificial lighting systems consisted of little more than sticks dipped into tar and set on fire. By 1800, the Scottish inventor William Murdock had developed a lamp that burned gas, and, before long, city dwellers throughout the civilized world had their own source of light. However, by the early twentieth century, many lighting systems were designed to operate on electricity.

Incandescent Lamps

The first widely successful electric light was the incandescent light, invented by Thomas Alva Edison in 1879. The term *incandescent* refers to an object that gives off light because it is heated. In an incandescent lamp, a wire filament is heated, begins to glow, and gives off both heat and light. Incandescent lights are now widely used, but they are not a very efficient way to produce artificial light. Less than ten percent of the electrical energy that enters an incandescent light bulb is transformed into light. The remaining 90 percent is converted to heat.

Neon Lamps

In the 1910s, the French chemist Georges Claude found another method for producing artificial light. Claude passed an electric current through a tube filled with a noble gas and found that the tube gave off a glow. This discovery marked the beginning of the lights we now know as neon lights. Many neon lights do, in fact, contain neon gas, but others contain different noble gases, such as argon, krypton, or xenon. Each of these gases gives off a distinctive color when electrical energy is passed through it. Thus, when you see a dramatic display of multicolored neon lights, each of the tubes contains a different gas.

Fluorescent Lamps

By the 1930s, scientists found that the inside surface of a neon lamp could be coated with a phosphorescent material that glows when struck by energy. Thus the fluorescent lamp was born. In a fluorescent lamp, an electric current flows from one end of the tube to the opposite end, exciting the mercury, argon, or krypton gas atoms within the tube. The energy given off by the excited gas atoms strikes the phosphor coating on the lamp, and the coating gives off a glow. The color of the glow depends on both the gas inside the lamp and the material used to coat the inside of the tube. Because most of the electrical energy supplied to them is converted to light, and relatively little to heat, fluorescent lamps are much more efficient than incandescent lamps.

Compact Fluorescent Lamps

The compact fluorescent lamp (CFL) was invented by Edward Hammer, an engineer, in 1976. Due to difficulty in manufacturing the lamp, CFLs were not commercially available until the early 1980s. They are designed to replace incandescent lamps and can fit into existing incandescent light fixtures. Compact fluorescent lamps are very popular because they use about one-quarter of the power of incandescent lamps of similar light output. CFLs also have an average lifespan between 8 and 15 times that of incandescent lamps. CFLs cost more than incandescent lamps, but the increase in cost is recovered in energy savings and replacement costs over the bulb's lifetime. However, like all fluorescent lamps, CFLs contain mercury. This makes safe disposal of CFLs complicated and causes a health risk if the lamp breaks.

Other Types of Lamps

Many variations on the incandescent and fluorescent lamp, as well as entirely different lamps, are available today. For example, an infrared lamp is a type of incandescent lamp that releases most of its energy in the infrared portion of the electromagnetic spectrum. This variation is achieved by modifying the temperature of the filament in the lamp. Whereas the filament in a typical 500-watt lamp is heated to about 2960 K, the filament in an infrared heat lamp is heated to only 2000 K. Infrared heat lamps are used for many purposes, such as drying paint, heating farm buildings, and treating muscles strains.

An ultraviolet lamp is a variation of a fluorescent lamp in which visible light is filtered out and only radiation in the ultraviolet portion of the spectrum (so-called "black light") is emitted. Lamps of this design are used for dramatic effect in advertising and decoration, as sunlamps, to destroy bacteria, and for the analysis of engineered products.

Some older forms of lamps now have only limited applications. For example, the carbon arc lamp, invented by Sir Humphry Davy in 1805, once had many industrial uses. The lamp operates by passing an electric current between two carbon electrodes. The electric current excites the gas between the two electrodes. The light given off comes partly from the excited gas molecules and partly from the glow of the hot carbon electrodes. Although carbon arc lamps have been largely replaced by high-intensity mercury vapor lamps, they are still used in projectors and searchlights, and in the fields of photography and scientific research.

Activity

What types of lighting systems do you encounter in your everyday life? Conduct a survey by making note of every light bulb or other artificial light source that you see over a three-day period. Make a table such as the one shown below for the lamps you find. If you discover a type of lamp not described above, refer to an encyclopedia or a physics textbook for further information about the operation and uses of the lamp.

Sample Report Form

Type of Lamp	Location(s)	Purpose(s)*	Advantage(s)
Incandescent	Rooms at home		Inexpensive, easy to change, provides sufficient light

*Indicate any purpose other than or in addition to providing light, such as for advertising, decoration, providing heat, and so on.

Name ______________________ Date ____________ Class ____________

CHAPTER 8

The Nitrogen Family: The Farmer's Best Friend

Background

The term agrochemical (or agrichemical) refers to any element or compound that is widely used in the field of agriculture. The most important groups of agrochemicals are probably synthetic fertilizers and pesticides. Synthetic agricultural chemicals include many compounds made from elements in Group 15, the nitrogen family.

Many different kinds of synthetic fertilizers are available, each one prepared for a particular kind of plant and a particular kind of growing environment. The primary nutrients included in most fertilizers are nitrogen (in the form of ammonia, urea, or some other nitrogen compound), phosphorus (usually as calcium dihydrogen phosphate), and potassium (usually as potassium chloride). The percentage of each nutrient is listed on the face of the fertilizer bag as a series of three numbers, such as 12-8-12. The sequence of the numbers refers to the percentage of nitrogen, diphosphorus pentoxide (P_2O_5), and potassium oxide (K_2O) present in the fertilizer.

A wide variety of pesticides are also available, each one designed for dealing with a particular pest in a particular environment. Many of these chemicals also contain elements in the nitrogen family. Naturally occurring compounds of arsenic were once widely used in pesticides, although they have now largely been replaced by other compounds.

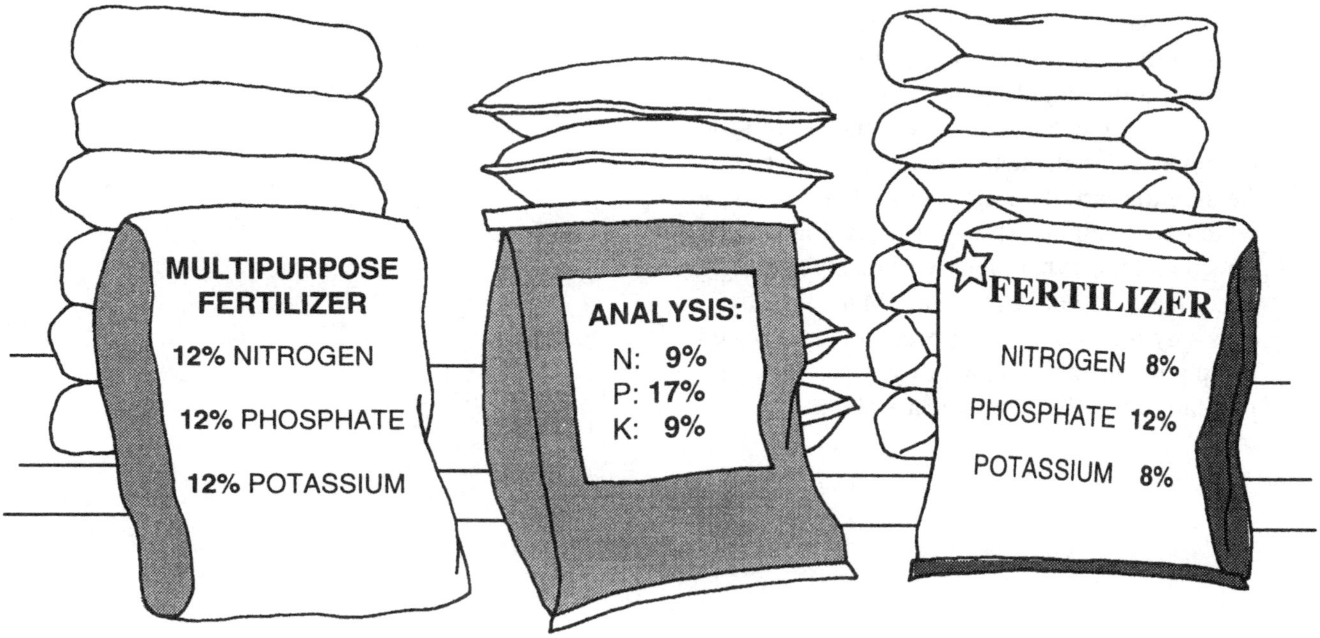

Survey

Visit any local store that sells agricultural supplies, such as a feed, seed, or gardening store. Ask the salesperson to show you a variety of fertilizers. Make a note of the composition and use of each. Note in particular the presence of elements in the nitrogen family as well as trace nutrients, or elements present in small quantities. Find out how a higher ratio of one nutrient contributes to a fertilizer's specific applications, such as for roses, root vegetables, African violets, or other plants.

Also see whether you can locate pesticides that contain arsenic, antimony, bismuth, or any other member of the nitrogen family. The salesperson can help you distinguish between inorganic pesticides that may contain these elements and organic pesticides, which usually do not.

Experiment

See whether you can detect any differences in the ways in which different fertilizers affect the growth of a particular kind of plant. Fill four small pots with a mixture of potting soil and fertilizer, using a different fertilizer for each of the four pots. Add exactly the same amount of fertilizer (about 1 g) to each pot, and mix it thoroughly with the potting soil. Put three seeds in each of the four pots. Use a fast-germinating seed, such as bean, corn, or pea. Be sure to mark the four pots so that you know which pot contains which fertilizer. Place the pots on a table where they will receive sunlight for at least six hours each day. Make sure the pots stay moist but do not become waterlogged. Keep a record of the changes you see in each pot daily until the seedlings are about 15 cm tall.

In making your selection of fertilizers, think of any way that you can conduct the experiment to test the effect of a specific nutrient. For example, a 6-18-20 fertilizer has twice as much potassium as 6-18-10 fertilizer. You can use these two fertilizers to examine the effect of doubling the amount of potassium used in soil. To the extent possible, set up the experiment in such a way as to permit a quantitative comparison among fertilizer effects.

Report

Outline a chemistry mini-unit on "The Nitrogen Family and Agrochemicals." The lesson should present the ways in which members of the nitrogen family and their compounds are used in fertilizers and pesticides. Prepare an outline that shows the concepts you would teach in such a unit and the teaching methods that would help students learn those concepts in an interesting way.

Present the results of your fertilizer experiment in a graph. You can use a simple bar graph to represent growth patterns in the four pots, or you can design a pictograph to show your results.

Name ________________ Date ________ Class ________

CHAPTER 9

Adhesives: Holding It All Together

Background

Adhesives have been used by humans almost from the beginning of recorded history. Records show that tar and pitch were used in the construction of buildings, a flour-and-water paste was used to bind papyrus, and simple animal glues were used to bind furniture parts to each other. These examples illustrate the use of natural products as adhesives. Since World War II, a new market in synthetic adhesives has propelled the U.S. adhesive businesses into a multi-billion dollar industry.

Today, a variety of adhesives are available for joining two objects made of the same or different materials. The different adhesives have been developed to meet a number of conditions, such as water resistance, low or high temperature, low or high electrical conductivity, and flexibility. As you can see in the illustration, today adhesives are even used in the construction of aircraft.

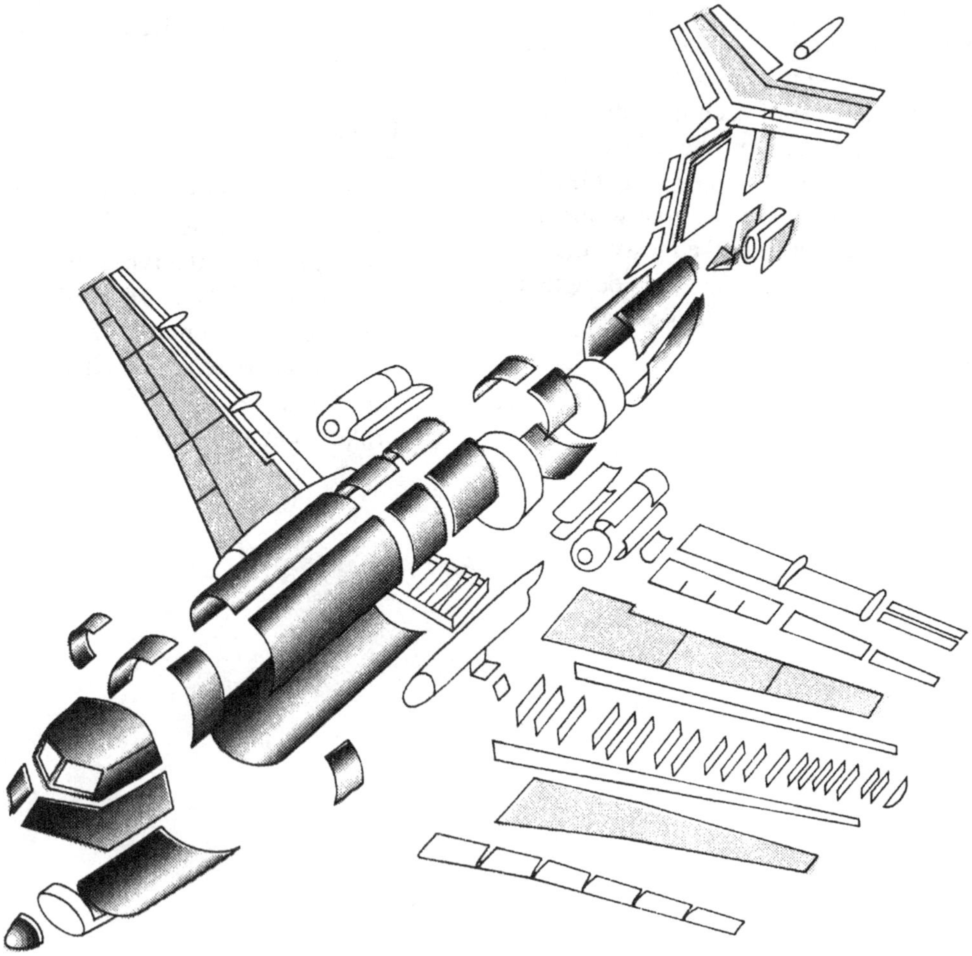

CHAPTER 9

Adhesives operate on one of two general principles: physical or chemical. Those of the former kind are usually solutions that form a bond between two materials when the water or other solvent they contain evaporates. Animal glues, for example, work because the water they contain evaporates upon standing, leaving behind a tough, hard material that sticks to objects to which it is attached. Chemical adhesives work because they undergo a chemical reaction to form bonds with the materials to which they are applied. For example, sodium silicate (Na_2SO_3; water glass) is used to make corrugated cardboard because it forms ionic bonds with negatively charged hydroxyl (OH^+) and positively charged hydrogen (H^-) groups in the paper of the cardboard.

Survey

Visit a hardware store and make a list of the different kinds of adhesives that are available there. For each product you find, make a note of the ingredients contained in the product and the purposes for which it is intended. Also try to find out what the role of each ingredient is. For example, is the ingredient the adhesive or the solvent, or does it have some other role? In terms of the adhesive's purpose, note whether the material is an "all-purpose" adhesive that is able to join any two materials, or is designed for only specific materials, such as wood, ceramics, plastics, or metal.

Experiment

Form an Adhesives Research Group with other members of your class. Research and design a series of experiments to show how well various adhesives work for particular materials and in various environmental conditions. Your group might research adhesives designed for woods, plastics, and ceramics. Group members might compare the effectiveness of specialized adhesives and all-purpose adhesives for the various materials.

Some of the questions your group might answer include the following.

1. Which of the adhesives held most tightly?
2. Which of the adhesives worked best under hot or cold conditions?
3. Which of the adhesives held well under moist conditions?
4. To what extent, if at all, was the strength of an adhesive affected by exposure to sunlight?

Report

When your group has completed its research, make a large poster that summarizes your results. Indicate the types of adhesives tested and the materials on which they were tested. Conclude your report with a series of recommendations as to which adhesives can be used for various household tasks, such as repairing broken pottery or joining pieces of wood.

Name ____________________ Date ____________ Class ____________

CHAPTER 10

Types of Glass

Background
Background
Background

Glass was first made as early as 1400 B.C. by the Egyptians. They heated a mixture of the naturally occurring mineral trona (a form of sodium carbonate), limestone, and sand to form calcium silicate, the simplest form of glass. Over the centuries, humans have discovered and invented many other variations of the basic Egyptian formula.

Today the term glass refers to a wide variety of materials that have in common a structure consisting primarily of a nonmetal oxide mixed with one or more metal oxides. In the case of the simple Egyptian formula, the nonmetal oxide is silicon dioxide (from sand), and the metal oxides are sodium oxide (from sodium carbonate) and calcium oxide (from limestone). The combination of these three substances results in the formation of glass, an interesting material that looks like a solid but is actually a super-cooled liquid.

Forms of glass differ from each other because different oxides are included in the mixture. The table below compares the composition of three types of glass used in different historical periods.

Type	% SiO_2	% CaO	% Na_2O	% Al_2O_3	% MgO	% Other
Egyptian	64	8	21	1.5	5	0.5 (K_2O)
Venetian	73	5	19	3	0	0
Quartz	100	0	0	0	0	0

In addition to the oxides described above, various kinds of glass also contain impurities, such as iron, manganese, chromium, and copper, that give them color. In some cases, the color occurs accidentally as a result of impurities present in the raw materials from which glass is made. However, these substances may also be added intentionally to obtain glasses of a particular color.

Activity

Today, you can purchase a number of different kinds of glass designed for many different purposes. The equipment that you use in your chemistry laboratory, for example, has been designed and made to deal with the special requirements of chemical experiments.

Listed below are a number of types of glass that are available today. Your task is to find out the composition of each type of glass and its use. A good source of information is a college chemistry textbook or a chemical reference book. You might also write about any other specialized type of glass that you come across in your research.

Some Forms of Glass

ceramic glass	photochromic glass
borosilicate glass	window glass
lead crystal glass	optical glass
safety glass	water glass

Report

After completing your research, select one type of glass for a more detailed report. You might choose an unusual type of glass, such as glass that is used to screen out neutrons, gamma rays, infrared radiation, or other forms of electromagnetic radiation. Or you might want to explore the way various types of glass have been developed for artistic purposes, such as the molding of glass statuary or decorative objects.

Name ______________________ Date ____________ Class ____________

Artificial Atmospheres

Background

The term artificial atmosphere refers to any system of gases that has been designed to serve some specific industrial, medical, personal, or other purpose. You probably already know about some artificial atmosphere systems although you don't think of them that way. For example, an oxygen mask used in hospitals and by emergency medical workers provides an artificial atmosphere. An oxygen mask delivers oxygen-rich air to patients who cannot breathe easily or whose lungs do not absorb oxygen well.

The gas in a lightbulb is also an artificial atmosphere. In manufacturing incandescent bulbs, for example, all of the air is pumped out of the light bulb. Then an unreactive gas, such as nitrogen or argon, is pumped into the bulb. If the bulb were filled with air, the metal filament that produces the light would react chemically with the air and break down.

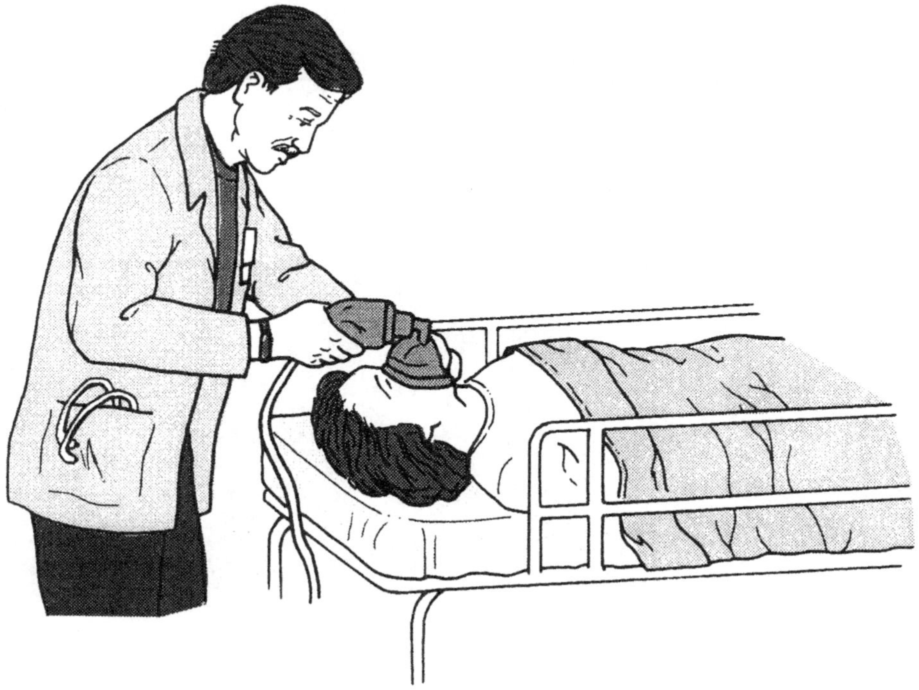

Name ______________________ Date ____________ Class ____________

CHAPTER 11

Activity

Your assignment is to learn more about one of the many artificial atmospheric systems. In some cases, you will be able to speak with an expert in the community who can explain how the system works. In other cases, you may have to consult a reference book to get the information you need. The table gives some suggestions.

Report

Your report should include a diagram or a working model of the artificial atmosphere system you chose. The diagram should show how gases move through the system, if they do, and any physical and chemical changes that take place within the system. You may be able to build a simple working model.

Some Artificial Atmospheres	
1. Scuba diving systems **2.** Diving bells used by nineteenth century explorers **3.** Deep-sea diving suits **4.** The gas that fills a fluorescent lightbulb **5.** The gas that fills a sodium-vapor lamp (used on highways) **6.** The atmospheric systems in U.S. and Soviet spacecrafts (They were different in the early years of the space programs of the two nations.)	**7.** The atmosphere in commercial jet airplanes **8.** Protective atmospheres used to preserve historic documents or fragile museum pieces **9.** Argon in high-temperature metallurgical processes **10.** "Clean" rooms and "negative-pressure" rooms for assembling delicate electronic equipment

Making STPP: Sodium Tripolyphosphate

Background

Detergents are some of the most common of all chemical products found in the American home. Almost every family has one or more kinds for washing clothes and dishes, or for more specialized jobs, such as cleaning tools. Yet few people realize that detergents are among the most complex chemical products in the home.

The key ingredient in a detergent is a surfactant, a material whose long, narrow molecules bond to grease and oil at one end and to water at the other end. Surfactants are good cleansing agents because they attach themselves to the oily surface that surrounds most dirt, and then carry away that dirt with the wash water. Possibly the best known of all surfactants is ordinary soap.

Detergents contain many chemicals other than surfactants, such as bleaches, fabric softeners, fragrances, optical brighteners, enzymes, fillers, foam stabilizers, and builders. Builders are the subject of this feature.

Surfactants by themselves often do not clean well in ordinary water because calcium and magnesium ions (Ca^{2+} and Mg^{2+}) interfere with the action of surfactant molecules. Builders bond to calcium and magnesium ions and allow the surfactant to do its cleaning job. The first builder used in a detergent was sodium tripolyphosphate ($Na_5P_3O_{10}$) in 1947.

Sodium tripolyphosphate, also known as STPP, was soon widely used in manufacturing detergents. Production reached 500 million kg by 1955 but peaked at 1.11 billion kg in 1970 because of concern that STPP (and other phosphates in detergents) might be harming lakes and ponds. In 1993, production was only 427 million kg and most STPP was used in detergents sold overseas, cold-water detergents, and detergents for dishwashers and institutional applications. Annual production averages 0.5 million kg in the United States with uses in electroplating and as corrosion inhibitors.

The series of reactions that produce sodium tripolyphosphate ($Na_5P_3O_{10}$) begins by the reaction of sulfuric acid (H_2SO_4) with a phosphate compound, usually calcium phosphate ($Ca_3(PO_4)_2$), to produce phosphoric acid (H_3PO_4).

$$Ca_3(PO_4)_2 + 3H_2SO_4 \rightarrow 3CaSO_4 + 2H_3PO_4$$

Then phosphoric acid and sodium carbonate (Na_2CO_3) react to form sodium dihydrogen phosphate (NaH_2PO_4) and sodium hydrogen phosphate (Na_2HPO_4), as shown in the two following equations.

$$2H_3PO_4 + Na_2CO_3 \rightarrow 2NaH_2PO_4 + H_2O + CO_2$$

$$H_3PO_4 + Na_2CO_3 \rightarrow Na_2HPO_4 + H_2O + CO_2$$

The amount of phosphoric acid and sodium carbonate is controlled so that a 1:2 mixture of sodium dihydrogen phosphate and sodium hydrogen phosphate is produced. This mixture is then heated to drive off water, producing sodium tripolyphosphate.

$$NaH_2PO_4 + 2Na_2HPO_4 \rightarrow Na_5P_3O_{10} + 2H_2O$$

Projects

The following are suggestions for further investigation.

1. Prepare a detailed report on the action of one component of detergents.
2. Research the effect of phosphates on the ecological balance of lakes and ponds.
3. Find out how cold-water detergents differ from other detergents and why their popularity has increased the demand for STPP.
4. Examine the list of ingredients on a package of detergent. Find out the purpose of each one.
5. About four percent of all STPP produced is used as a food additive. Find out why.

Name ______________________ Date ____________ Class ____________

CHAPTER 13

A Hard Day at the Laundromat

Background

Television advertisements sometimes warn consumers about the problems posed by "hard" water. That term applies to water in which it is difficult to make suds. Hard water can be a problem for consumers because some of the soap added to a washing machine goes into softening the hard water in the machine. Anyone who washes clothes in hard water is therefore throwing away some of the soap he or she buys for laundry day.

Hard water is caused primarily by the presence of Ca^{2+} and Mg^{2+} ions in water. When a river flows over the ground, it dissolves some of the minerals over which it passes, minerals such as compounds of magnesium and calcium. The compounds remain in solution when the water is taken by a municipal water system for transfer to businesses and residences.

When soap is added to such water, a reaction takes place between the soap (typically sodium stearate, $NaC_{18}H_{35}O_2$) and calcium and magnesium ions in the water. The products of this reaction are insoluble compounds, the scum that forms on the top of hard water when soap is added to it. A typical reaction is as follows:

$$NaC_{18}H_{35}O_2(aq) + Ca^{2+}(aq) \rightarrow 2Na^{+}(aq) + Ca(C_{18}H_{35}O_2)_2(s)$$

When water is softened, calcium and magnesium ions are removed. Then, when soap is added to the softened water, it can all be used to form suds and clean clothes, and none of it is wasted on softening the water first.

Activity

A number of methods are available for softening water. The method selected by a company or a family will depend on a number of factors, including the amount of water to be softened and the cost. In order to find out more about water-softening devices that are available, arrange a visit with a local company that specializes in that line of work. Ask to speak with a manager or salesperson. Have that person demonstrate for you one or more systems for softening water, and ask her or him to explain the chemical principles on which the system works. Ask for a before-and-after demonstration that shows the results of softening water.

Experiment

A simple method for softening hard water makes use of common washing soda (sodium carbonate). Begin this experiment by preparing your own sample of hard water. Add 5 g of Epsom salts (magnesium sulfate) to 250 mL of distilled water in a beaker. Stir, and then allow the solution to stand for 10 minutes. At the end of the time, pour the clear upper part of the solution into the beaker, and you will have a sample of hard water.

To test the hardness of this water, use any commercial brand of liquid soap. Do not use detergent. With a medicine dropper or pipette, add liquid soap to 100 mL of the hard water, shaking the mixture well after every fifth drop. Watch for the formation of a scum, which is the calcium stearate precipitate. When all calcium ions have been precipitated out, the liquid soap you add will begin to make suds. Count the number of drops needed to produce suds that will last 1 minute. Record this number as an indication of the hardness of the water you made.

To soften your sample of hard water, add 1 g of washing soda (sodium carbonate) to 100 mL of the hard water. Stir well until all the washing soda has dissolved. Now repeat the test described above with liquid soap, adding one drop at a time and noting the number of drops needed to obtain lasting suds. Compare the amount of soap added to the softened water to the amount needed for the hard water. Invent a scale for indicating the hardness of water, based on the number of soap drops needed to make suds.

Finally, collect water samples from at least three different locations around your area. Perform the liquid-soap test described above on each sample to determine its hardness. Rate each sample of water according to the scale for hardness that you developed.

Report

Pretend that you are a salesperson for a water-softening company. Your job is to convince the owners of a small, five-bedroom bed-and-breakfast inn that they should install a water softening unit in their inn. Write a speech that you would give explaining why such a unit would be useful and how it would operate. Think of ways to make your speech interesting and convincing by using materials such as tables, charts, diagrams, and illustrations.

Name ______________________ Date ______________ Class ______________

CHAPTER 14

Adding Spice to Your Daily Diet: Acidulants as Food Additives

Background

An important commercial application of acids is as food additives. Acids are added to foods primarily for three reasons: as flavor enhancers, as preservatives, and as antioxidants. When used as food additives, acids are known as acidulants.

Various acids are used to enhance flavor because of the tart, fruit-like taste they give to foods. Citrus acid is added to provide a lemon- or lime-like flavor, malic acid for an apple flavor, acetic acid for a vinegar taste, and tartaric acid for a grape-like flavor. Soft drinks, gelatin desserts, and pie fillings get their tart flavor from fumaric, phosphoric, and other acids.

Acids also help to prevent foods from spoiling because they provide an acidic environment in which bacteria do not survive well. In addition to the acids mentioned above, adipic, ascorbic, lactic, and other acids are effective as food preservatives. Acids that contain two acid groups, such as citric acid, act as antioxidants because the two acidic groups work together to trap metal ions that cause foods to go rancid and develop bad odors.

Survey

Which acids are used as food additives? What foods contain these acids? You can answer these questions by visiting a local grocery store and surveying some of the food products found there. You may want to talk with the manager before you begin your survey. For this research, focus on just two aisles at the store,—the one in which canned fruits and vegetables are kept and the one where beverages are found. Look at any twenty products in each aisle. Keep a record of each product that contains an acid as a food additive. You can obtain this information from the list of ingredients on the can or jar label.

Summarize the results of your survey by making a table that lists every acidulant found and the products in which it was contained. Based on the nature of the product, see if you can hypothesize the reason that the acid was used in each particular product.

Research

How effective are acids as flavor enhancers? You can investigate this question by carrying out some simple experiments. The instructions that follow provide some general guidelines for the kind of experiments you can do. Think of some variations that might deal with other questions that interest you. But do not conduct any experiments without first receiving approval from your instructor.

As you may know, tasting is normally not an accepted test in the chemistry laboratory. Too many chemicals are dangerous to allow such a test. However, the chemicals selected for this experiment have been chosen because of their safety. To be completely safe, do not conduct any of the following experiments until your teacher has examined your setup and given approval for you to continue.

Ask your teacher to prepare a five percent solution of citric acid in water. This solution will be the *Test Solution* used in this experiment. Select five volunteer tasters for your experiment. Give each taster a glass of tap water to taste. Do not tell them what liquid they are tasting. Ask them to describe to you the taste of the liquid. You would expect them *not* to mention any acidic or tart flavor in the tap water, but make a note of any comment that differs from a simple "water" flavor mentioned by your testers.

Now prepare three different solutions from the five percent citric acid Test Solution. Be sure your teacher approves these solutions for tasting. Solution A should consist of 10 mL of the Test Solution in 100 mL of distilled water. What is the concentration of this solution? Solution B should consist of 10 mL of Solution A in 100 mL of distilled water. What is the concentration of this solution? Solution C should consist of 10 mL of Solution B in 100 mL of distilled water. What is the concentration of this solution?

Ask your five tasters to take a drink of Solution C and describe its flavor to you. Repeat the test with Solution B and then Solution A. At what point does each taster report the presence of a tart or acidic flavor? What conclusions can you draw from this experiment?

Report

Write a report describing your experiment and the results you obtained. First list the variables you tested in the experiment. Then describe the steps you followed in carrying out your experiment. Next, summarize the results you obtained in the experiment. Finally, write a paragraph that explains how an experiment of this kind might be of value to a food processing company.

Name ______________________ Date ______________ Class ______________

CHAPTER 15

pH in the pHlower Garden

Background

Many factors affect the growth of plants: light, moisture, and nutrients are a few. Acidity is another. One reason why acidity affects growth rate is because pH can influence the efficiency with which various nutrients are released from the soil.

Most soils tend to be slightly acidic because of the rainwater that percolates through them. Rainwater contains carbonic acid, formed when carbon dioxide in the atmosphere dissolves in water and reacts with it. However, if soils contain lime or other basic rocks and minerals, the soils tend to be less acidic, or they may even be basic. The reason is that the calcium oxide or calcium hydroxide in lime react with carbonic acid and neutralize it. These reactions can be summarized as follows:

$$CaO + H_2CO_3 \rightarrow H_2O + CaCO_3$$

$$Ca(OH)_2 + H_2CO_3 \rightarrow 2H_2O + CaCO_3$$

Various kinds of plants grow better in soil of different pH ranges. Most grow well in either mildly acidic or mildly basic soils but are damaged by extremes of pH. Camellias, rhododendrons, and azaleas are examples of plants that do especially well in acidic soil but do very poorly in alkaline soils.

Many home gardeners regularly test the pH value of their soil and make the adjustments necessary for the plants they grow. Soils that are too basic can be improved by adding peat moss, ground bark, sawdust, or high-acid fertilizers. Soils that are too acidic can be modified by adding lime.

CHAPTER 15

Experiment 1

Testing for the pH of soil is a simple procedure that you can do with a commercial soil testing kit, available at any garden store, or with universal indicator paper, available from your chemistry teacher. To carry out this test, begin by finding samples of about five different soil types: clay, sandy, loamy, etc. If you use a commercial soil testing kit, follow the directions on the label for finding the pH of each soil sample. If you use indicator paper to find pH, first place about 5 g of each soil type into separate test tubes. Then add enough distilled water to nearly fill each of your 5 tubes. Shake the test tubes vigorously for about a minute; then place one drop of liquid from each tube on the indicator paper. Compare the color of the paper with the chart on the indicator package and record the pH of the soils in the test tubes.

Experiment 2

Soils that are too acidic for a particular crop can be neutralized by the addition of lime. To see how this process works, use the same 5 test tubes from Experiment 1 above. Prepare a neutralizing solution by adding about 1 g of slaked lime (calcium oxide) or powdered lime (calcium hydroxide) to 100 mL of water and shake well. Filter the solution, and then use the filtrate to neutralize the soil samples in the 5 test tubes. Drop a piece of indicator paper into the first test tube and then add the lime solution drop by drop until the indicator paper indicates a pH of 7.0. Record the number of drops needed to neutralize this solution. Repeat this procedure with each of the soils that you found to be acidic in Experiment 1.

Report

Prepare a table that summarizes the results of your experiments. The table should list each type of soil you tested and its pH. Then list the number of drops of lime solution needed to neutralize each of the acidic soils. What relationship exists between the acidity of a soil and the amount of lime solution needed to neutralize that soil?

Name ______________________ Date __________ Class __________

CHAPTER 16

What a Rotten Apple: Food Preservation Techniques

Background

Most foods begin to spoil almost from the moment they are harvested. The two most common reasons for spoilage are the actions of bacteria, fungi, and other microorganisms, and oxidation. In either of these cases, a healthful product is converted into a form that is distasteful, at least, and toxic, at worst. Because most foods today travel from farm to grocery store to home over a period of days or weeks, the prevention of food spoilage is a major concern to food producers and processors.

Over the centuries, humans have devised a number of techniques for preventing food spoilage. These include drying, smoking, curing, freezing, canning, cooling, pasteurizing, and adding chemicals. Most of these techniques work because they produce an environment in which bacteria and other microorganisms do not survive. The addition of chemicals may accomplish the same goal, or it may attack the second cause of food spoilage, oxidation.

Part One

Listed in the table are a number of chemicals that are added to foods to prevent them from spoiling. Consult a college textbook, a book on food additives, or another resource that will describe the way in which each chemical prevents food from spoiling and the kinds of food in which it is used. With this information, complete the table.

Chemical	Mechanism	Uses/Foods Used In
Salt (NaCl)		
$NaNO_2$		
Sorbic acid		
Citric acid		
Ascorbic acid		
BHA and BHT		
Propyl gallate		

Part Two

How well will citric acid prevent the spoilage of fruit juice? The following experiment will help you find an answer to that question. Begin with 50 mL of fresh-squeezed apple juice that is divided into five equal portions. Place each portion into a clean baby-food jar with a tight-fitting lid. Label the jars *A, B, C, D*, and *E*.

Make a 10% solution of citric acid by adding 10 g of crystalline citric acid to 100 mL of distilled water. Label this *Solution A*. From the 10%t citric acid solution, make four additional solutions, as follows. Make a 1% citric acid solution by mixing 10 mL of Solution A with 90 mL of distilled water. Label this *Solution B*. Mix 10 mL of Solution B with 90 mL of distilled water and label this *Solution C*. Mix 10 mL of Solution C with 90 mL of distilled water and label this *Solution D*. Finally, mix 10 mL of Solution D with 90 mL of distilled water and label this *Solution E*.

To jar A of apple juice, add 10 drops of Solution A. Add 10 drops of Solution B to jar B, 10 drops of Solution C to jar C, 10 drops of Solution D to jar D, and 10 drops of Solution E to jar E. Place the jars at room temperature in a dry place where you can observe them each day. Look for signs that the apple juice has begun to spoil. Keep a record of the effectiveness of each solution of citric acid as a preservative for the apple juice.

Report

1. In the space below, describe the evidence of spoilage you were able to observe in this experiment.

______

______

______

______

______

______

______

2. In the table below, indicate the day ("Day 1," "Day 2," etc.) on which evidence of spoilage could be observed in each jar.

Jar	Day on Which Spoilage Was First Observed
A	
B	
C	
D	
E	

3. Write a paragraph that summarizes what you learned about the effectiveness of citric acid as a preservative for apple juice. Then design a new experiment that could be used to test the effectiveness of some other chemical as a preservative for another type of food. Incorporate into your experimental design any modifications in the citric acid experiment you could suggest based on the results of your experiment.

Name ______________________ Date ____________ Class ____________

CHAPTER 17

What's new in batteries?

Background

If you've ever wanted to be an inventor, you might want to think about batteries. Scientists are constantly looking for new ways to build voltaic cells. They want voltaic cells that can be used to produce electrical current for a variety of purposes at reasonable cost with limited impact on the environment. Here are a few ideas that have been suggested.

The sodium-sulfur battery: The sodium-sulfur battery has an anode of molten sodium and a cathode of molten sulfur and molten sodium polysulfide (Na_2S_x). The two electrodes are separated from each other by a ceramic barrier that allows sodium ions to flow from the anode to the cathode. The half-reactions that take place in the cell are as follows.

anode: $Na^0 \rightarrow Na^+ + e^-$

cathode: $S^0 + 2e^- \rightarrow S^{2-}$

The battery can be recharged by passing an electric current through it, reforming elemental sodium and sulfur. Because the sodium and sulfur are both molten, sodium-sulfur batteries must operate at 300-350°C and can produce as much power as 60 kilowatts per hour. Sodium-sulfur batteries have possible energy storage applications for renewable energy at wind farms and solar energy plants.

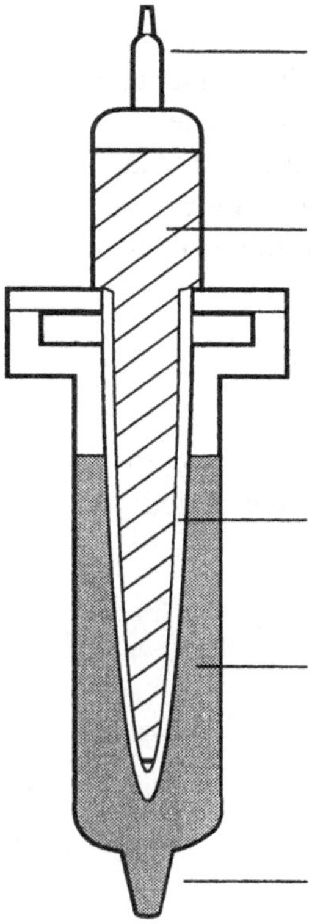

Solid-state batteries: A solid-state battery consists of a solid block of material used as an anode and a second block of material used as a cathode, with the two blocks separated by a third block of solid electrolyte. The anode might be made of an aluminum-lithium alloy and the cathode might be made of titanium disulfide (TiS_2). The electrolyte could be a crystalline material.

As lithium atoms lose electrons to become ions, they migrate through the electrolyte into the solid titanium disulfide. There, they fit neatly into pockets in layers of the TiS_2. Electrons released at the anode travel through the external circuit, where they are available to do any work that can be done by an electric current. Then they return to the cell at the cathode. At the cathode, lithium ions trapped in the TiS_2 layers pick up electrons and become lithium atoms. Some pacemaker devices implanted in the chest of heart-disease patients use solid-state batteries, as do cameras, watches, and calculators.

Plastic batteries: You may usually think of plastics as nonconductors. However, in the 1970s scientists discovered that some plastics can become electrically conductive and, under the right conditions, can conduct an electrical current nearly as well as a metal. The first such plastic to be discovered was polyacetylene. Polyacetylene contains many electrons that are not tightly bound to the molecule. They can be passed along from one part of the molecule to another, resulting in a small electrical current. Adding small amounts of iodine can increase the conductivity more than a trillion times. Iodine atoms, which contain seven valence electrons, readily attract an eighth electron to their outer energy level. Iodine atoms added to the polyacetylene molecule greatly promote the movement of electrons along the molecule, causing electrical current to flow through it.

Because polyacetylene is like other plastics in many ways—it can be made into thin, flexible sheets or strips—a battery made of polyacetylene might look different from the lead storage batteries and dry cells you are familiar with. For example, automobile engineers have designed cars in which polyacetylene is used to cover the body of the car. Rather than hiding the battery under the car's hood, they have made the battery a part of the car body itself.

However, polyacetylene is brittle, difficult to produce, chemically stable only in liquid solutions, and it degrades in air. Researchers continue to develop more suitable plastics for batteries, such as polyaniline, which is inexpensive and stable in both water and air.

Exercise

What kinds of batteries are for sale in your community? Visit a local hardware store and an auto supply store to see what kinds of batteries you can find. Make a list of the types of batteries and note the names of any chemicals listed on the battery label or package.

Select one of the battery types you found. Research the battery and make a diagram to explain how it works. Identify the anode, cathode, and electrolyte. Trace the flow of electrical current through the battery. Write the half-reactions that occur at each electrode. List the advantages and disadvantages of this type of battery. Consult college textbooks in chemistry or other resource materials for additional information.

Name ______________________ Date ____________ Class ____________

CHAPTER 18

A More Beautiful You ... Thanks to Chemistry

Background

The use of chemicals to improve one's personal appearance is hardly a new phenomenon. Records indicate that Egyptian women used a compound of antimony to darken their eyes as early as the fourth millenium B.C. A green eye shadow made of copper ore goes back even further, perhaps to as early as 5000 B.C.

Chemists are still working today to find ways of making skin smoother, hair more lustrous, teeth more sparkling, nails more attractive, and general appearance more appealing. The cosmetic and health-care products that you find on pharmacy and grocery shelves today represent a fascinating application of improved chemical know-how and powerful marketing techniques.

Most of the products that you can buy today were made on the basis of some simple physical and chemical principles. The following experiments will illustrate for you the ease with which useful personal-care products can be made.

Experiment 1

The product known as cold cream is used to remove makeup and to keep skin clean and moist. It consists primarily of two raw materials: white beeswax and mineral oil. To make your own cold cream, you will need to use a water bath. Ask your instructor to show you how to set up a water bath and then to observe you as you carry out this experiment.

Add about 50 g of white beeswax and 250 mL of mineral oil to a large beaker, and set the beaker in a water bath on a hot plate. Heat the mixture gently until the beeswax melts and dissolves. In a separate beaker, very carefully add 100 mL of boiling water to 10 g of borax. Stir until the borax dissolves completely. Carefully add the hot borax solution to the beeswax/mineral-oil solution while stirring constantly. You can impart a color and an odor to the cold cream, if you wish, by adding a drop of food coloring and of perfume to the cold-cream mixture.

Observe what happens as the mixture is allowed to cool. When it has cooled completely, add a portion of the mixture about the size of a small pea to the back of your hand, and describe its feeling.

With a small variation, you can use the above recipe to make lipstick. Color and texture are the major differences between lipstick and cold cream: lipstick has a bright color and a firmer texture than cold cream does. To get a more solid consistency, change the composition of the original mixture to equal amounts of beeswax and mineral oil; for example, 100 g beeswax and 100 mL oil. Again, use caution when working with the water bath. You can add color to your lipstick when the beeswax/mineral-oil combination is being heated by adding a few drops of food coloring or a few shavings from a crayon that is marked "nontoxic."

While the beeswax/mineral-oil mixture is cooling, make a mold for your lipstick out of aluminum foil. Wrap a piece of heavy-duty aluminum foil around a small test tube, then remove the foil. Be sure the foil mold is sealed at the bottom. When the beeswax/mineral-oil mixture is cool enough to handle but still liquid, pour it into the aluminum foil mold. After the lipstick hardens, test it on the back of your hand. What do you think of its color and texture?

Experiment 2

Many personal-care products are designed to improve not just appearance, but also health. A mouthwash, for example, is designed not only to prevent bad breath, but also to kill bacteria that may cause dental problems. How effective are mouthwashes in performing this second task?

You can make a simple home-remedy mouthwash as follows. Add a pinch of zinc chloride, 5 g of borax, and 10 g of sodium hydrogen carbonate to 250 mL of distilled water in a beaker. Stir the mixture thoroughly until all the ingredients have dissolved. **WARNING: *Do not attempt to use this mouthwash*.** It is to be used only to test the bacteria-killing ability of a popular commercial recipe for mouthwashes.

Sterilize two petri dishes by heating them in a 200°C oven for one hour. Label the lid of one dish *A* and the other dish *B*. Pour enough melted nutrient agar solution into each petri dish to cover the bottom of the dish, and leave the cover off both dishes for about 15 minutes. This will allow time for bacteria in the air to settle on the agar surface and begin to multiply. If necessary, ask your instructor for further assistance in preparing the petri dishes needed in this experiment.

Add several drops of mouthwash to dish *A* and spread it over the surface using a cotton swab. Or alternatively, soak several filter paper disks in the mouthwash and place them on the agar surface. Cover the dish. Add nothing to the agar in dish *B*, and cover it also. Incubate the dishes upside down (unless using disks). Check both dishes at least once a day for the next week to see what changes have occurred.

The procedure you have used in this mouthwash test can be used for commercial products also. Simply repeat the test, using the commercial product instead of your home-made mouthwash. Develop a quantitative way of comparing the effectiveness of the mouthwashes you test.

Survey and Report

Conduct a survey of local stores to compare personal-care products. Make a list of all the brands of cold cream or mouthwash. Check the list of ingredients to see how the brands differ from each other in composition. Also compare the prices of the brands you find.

Write a short market survey of the products you have studied. How do the various brands differ from each other, and why might one be preferred over the others? As far as is possible, determine whether the differences in price among brands are justified by differences in the products themselves. Write a report of your findings.

Name ______________________ Date ____________ Class ____________

CHAPTER 19

Cooking Chemistry

Background

For most people, cooking is a skill that develops after a great deal of practice. Scientific principles are involved in the process of cooking, however, to a much greater degree than most people recognize. Knowing something about the chemistry of cooking can actually add considerably to a chef's skills.

The baking of dishes that contain eggs is an example. The first thing that occurs when an egg is heated is that protein molecules in the egg become denatured; that is, they uncoil and lose their characteristic three-dimensional shape. Next, the egg proteins coagulate by forming cross-links, and they form a lumpy mass. The precise way in which these changes take place depends on a number of factors, including how vigorously the eggs are stirred, how rapidly and to what temperature they are heated, and what other ingredients are included with them in a recipe.

Activity 1

You can test some of the scientific factors involved in cooking by making a simple custard. A custard is a mixture of eggs, milk, sugar, and flavoring. The mixture is baked in a water bath in a moderate oven (325°F–350°F) until the mixture sets (becomes firm). Refer to any basic cookbook for the instructions for making a custard, or use the recipe below. Then, think about the ways in which that recipe could be altered to test for the effects of stirring, heating rate, temperature, and added ingredients.

Working in a group that includes three other students, design experiments to test those factors.

In the table on the next page, state the ways in which the tests will be carried out. Then, each member of the group should carry out one of the tests. Record the results. Work under adult supervision and be careful not to burn yourself. Do not eat the custard because of the danger of undercooking or contamination.

Recipes

Baked Custard

3 slightly beaten eggs
1/4 cup sugar
1/4 teaspoon salt
2 cups milk, near boiling
1/2 teaspoon vanilla

Combine eggs, sugar, and salt. Slowly stir in slightly cooled milk and vanilla. Set six 5-ounce custard cups in shallow pan on oven rack. Pour hot water around them, 1 inch deep. Pour in custard. Bake in 325° F oven 40 to 45 minutes, or until knife inserted off-center comes out clean. Serve warm or chilled.

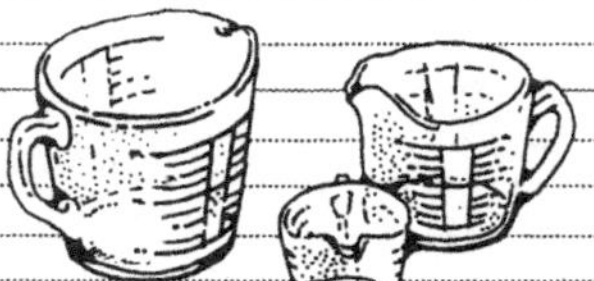

Factor	Method of Testing
Stirring	
Heating rate	
Temperature	
Added ingredients	

Activity 2

As an extension of the above activity, consider the problem of preparing the two dishes, crème anglaise and crème patissière (pastry cream). The only difference between the two recipes is the use of flour or cornstarch in the latter. The presence of the flour or cornstarch in crème patissière has a significant effect on the preparation and appearance of the product. The reason for this effect is that the polysaccharide molecules in the flour or cornstarch prevent denatured egg proteins from forming the cross-links that would cause them to coagulate.

Find recipes for the preparation of each of these two dishes and design modifications that will allow you to observe the effect of adding the polysaccharide to one recipe and not to the other. Once again, work under adult supervision, be careful not to burn yourself, and do not eat the finished product.

Report

The report for these two activities should include a showing of the final products of your baking experience. Accompany each display with a 3" × 5" card that briefly summarizes the chemical principles illustrated by the preparation and appearance of the product.

Name ______________________ Date ____________ Class ____________

CHAPTER 20

Energy from Solid Wastes

Background

Two problems with which many cities have to deal today are how to get rid of solid wastes and how to obtain energy. Incinerating waste can solve both of these problems at once, although not without creating some other problems.

A typical solid-waste incineration process includes the following major steps.

1. Wastes are delivered to the incineration plant and placed in a precombustion chamber for drying, ignition, and partial burning.
2. The material, much of which has not completely burned, drops onto a moving grate and is carried to the major combustion chamber, which is at a higher temperature than the precombustion chamber. There, the burning process is completed. Any unburned gases from the first chamber are also passed through the major combustion chamber and burned.
3. Heat from the combustion chamber is used to boil water. The steam formed in the boiler is piped to a site where it is used for heating or to generate electricity.
4. Gaseous combustion products formed when the wastes burn are cooled and vented to the atmosphere after particulates are removed by dust collectors. These gases must be released according to Environmental Protection Agency (EPA) standards for clean air.
5. Ashes and noncombustible solid materials remaining after passage through the major combustion chamber are cooled and then trucked to a landfill. These solids are usually about 10 percent of the waste.

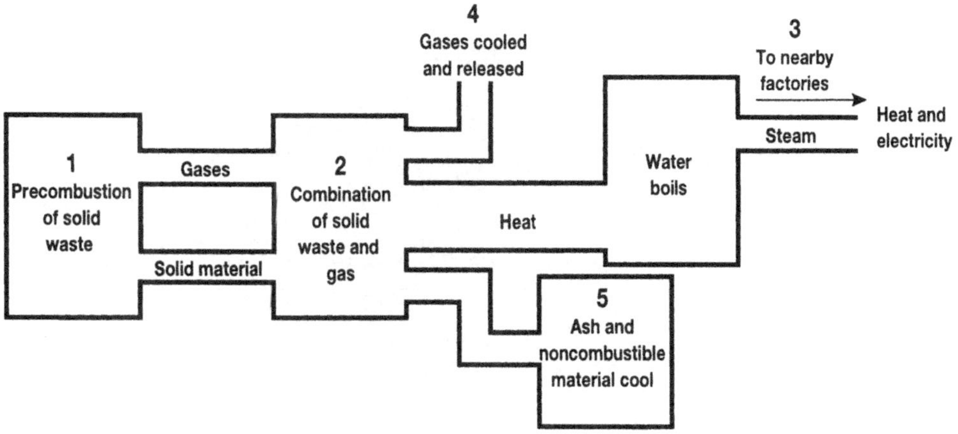

CHAPTER 20

Activity

The incineration of wastes may sound like a relatively simple and efficient way to get rid of solid wastes and to produce energy at the same time, but the process is more complex than it sounds. In addition, many people object for environmental reasons to incineration as a means of waste disposal. In this activity, you should speak with some individuals who support incineration as well as with some who oppose it. Some of the people you might contact include the following.

1. A local government official responsible for waste disposal or one who is responsible for protecting the local environment
2. A member of a conservation or environmental group, such as the Sierra Club, the League of Conservation Voters, or the Student Conservation Association
3. Someone who works for a waste disposal company
4. One or more interested citizens, such as someone from your family or your neighborhood

If your city or town already has a waste disposal incinerator, try to find out what people think of the incinerator, what objections they have to it, what advantages they see, and what recommendations they would make to other communities exploring waste incineration. If your community does not have a waste incinerator, ask residents what arguments in favor of and against the construction of such a plant in your community might be.

Report

Your report for this activity should list all the pro and con arguments of incineration as well as counter arguments to each objection. Include your own views on incinerating solid wastes. Support your position with the arguments you have cited.

Name ______________________ Date ____________ Class ____________

CHAPTER 21

Medical Uses of Radioisotopes

Background

Radioactive isotopes have a host of applications in the medical sciences, sometimes for therapeutic purposes (treating a medical problem) and sometimes for diagnostic purposes (finding out more about a medical problem). An example of the first application is the treatment of some forms of cancer with cobalt-60. This radioisotope gives off gamma rays, which can kill cancer cells.

Radioisotopes are used as tracers in diagnosis. A tracer is a substance whose location and movement can easily be observed. Suppose solution of sodium chloride containing radioactive sodium-24 is injected into a patient's blood-stream. As the radioisotope travels through the body, it gives off beta and gamma radiation, which can be detected by a particle counter suspended over the body.

Technetium-99m

One of the most commonly used radioisotopes for diagnostic purposes is technetium-99m. The letter m stands for metastable, meaning that the isotope gives off energy and becomes a more stable form of the element. Technetium-99m has a half-life of 6.02 hours. The isotope decays to technetium-99, with a half-life of 212 000 years.

Technetium-99m is used to study liver, spleen, kidney, and lung function. The technetium is converted into the pertechnitate ion (TcO_4^-), which then accumulates in the organ to be studied.

Technetium-99m has several advantages for diagnosis. First, the radioisotope has a half-life long enough to allow a physician to inject it into the body and to follow its progress for a substantial period of time. However, its half-life is short enough so that it does not remain in the body for a long time, giving off harmful gamma radiation. Also, technetium-99m gives off only gamma radiation, meaning that no alpha or beta radiation is present to cause additional damage to healthy tissue during the test.

The short half-life of technetium-99m also presents a problem. Suppose the isotope had to be made in a nuclear reactor and then shipped to a hospital a few hundred miles away. By the time the isotope arrived at the hospital, most of it would have decayed to the more stable and less useful technetium-99. Scientists have found an intriguing solution to this problem. They use a nuclear reactor to produce a radioactive isotope of molybdenum, technetium's next door neighbor in the periodic table. The half-life of molybdenum-99 is 67 hours. It decays, by emitting a beta particle, to technetium-99m. The molybdenum-99 can be made at one location and then shipped hundreds of miles away without having decayed substantially.

When molybdenum-99 is prepared for medical use, it is sealed in a lead container, called a molybdenum-99 "cow," and then sent to a hospital or clinic. At the medical facility, a doctor or technician can "milk the cow" by washing out its container with a saline (sodium chloride) solution. The saline solution that comes out of the cow contains technetium-99m, produced by the following nuclear reaction.

$$^{99}_{42}\text{Mo} \longrightarrow {}^{99}_{43}\text{Tc} + {}^{\ 0}_{-1}\text{e}$$

The technetium-99m is now ready for medical use.

Name ______________________ Date ____________ Class ____________

CHAPTER 21

Exercise

Some of the other radioisotopes used for medical diagnosis are listed to the right. Find a technician, nurse, or physician who will talk to you about the uses of each one or use an introductory chemistry text for nurses or an organic chemistry text.

Radioisotope	Uses
Chromium-54	
Gallium-67	
Iodine-131	
Phosphorus-32	
Sodium-24	
Thallium-201	

1 Alloys: When Mixtures Are Better Than Pure Substances

Research

- Compositions of most alloys vary significantly. The answers given for the chart are only suggestive of the composition of alloys.

Some Common Alloys: Their Compositions

Alloy	Composition (percent by mass)	Use
Dental amalgam	Hg: 50; Ag: 35; Sn: 13; Cu: 1.5; Zn: 0.5	dental fillings
Cast iron	Fe: 96; C: 4	castings
Coinage metal	Cu: 75; Ni: 25	U.S. coin composition
Electronic solder	Pb: 37; Sn: 63	affixing electrical conductors to each other (not plumber's solder)
Monel	Ni: 60; Cu: 33; Fe: 7	corrosion-resistant containers
Nichrome	Ni: 80–85; Cr: 15–20	heating elements
Pewter	Sn: 85–92; Sb: 1–5; Bi; Cu, Pb: balance	decorative tableware
Type metal	Pb: 70; Sb: 18; Sn: 10; Cu: 2	printer's type
Wood's metal	Bi: 50; Pb: 25; Sn: 12.5; Cd: 12.5	automatic sprinkling systems

Activity

- Provide students with alloy samples that will be small enough to fit into a 100 mL graduated cylinder.
- Select a variety of common alloys, such as brass, bronze, stainless steel, and Wood's metal.
- You may want to offer students more than one form of the more common alloys mentioned in note 2 to indicate that bronze, brass, stainless steel, and other alloys occur with different compositions and, therefore, different physical properties.
- In predicting possible uses for the alloys studied, students might mention applications, such as jewelry and objects of art because of color and/or luster, or a construction material for alloys of low density but high strength.
- As an extension, you can demonstrate other physical properties of alloys, such as conductivity of heat and melting point (for low-melting point alloys).

2 Cathode Ray Tubes

The five major parts of the cathode ray tube or television picture tube are the electron gun, the focusing system, the deflection system, the display screen, and the container (or envelope). You may want to ask students to explore the use of cathode ray tubes in other applications, such as radar, the oscilloscope, large-screen display, and storage tubes.

3 Keeping Swimming Pools Clean

Part One

Rather than talking to a manager, students can find information on chlorination by searching the Internet.

1. It might be added in the elemental form, as chlorine gas, or as a hypochlorite [NaOCl or $Ca(OCl)_2$].
2. Most commercial pools operate on an automatic chlorinating system to which chemicals must be added at certain periods of time. Spas are often chlorinated daily.
3. The most common tests are for chlorine level, pH, alkalinity, and cyanuric acid.
4. You may find that some system other than chlorination is used to ensure the purity of pool water. For example, bromination, rather than chlorination, is sometimes used. If the pool visit uses some other form of purification, ask the same questions about that system.

Part Two

Answers to the questions for Part Two will vary from town to town and county to county.

Part Three

1. $Cl_2 + H_2O \rightarrow HCl + HClO$
2. Sodium hypochlorite or calcium hypochlorite dissolves in water to release sodium ions and hypochlorite ions or calcium ions and hypochlorite ions, respectively.
3. Various answers are possible. One involves the reaction between chlorine and ortho-tolidine to give a pink color that changes in intensity depending on the level chlorine.

4 How Noble, Those Gases!

Some possible uses for the noble gases are as follows:

- helium: production of low temperatures, balloons and airships, lasers, diluent for gases, rocket research, metallurgical work such as welding;
- neon: "neon" light, fillers in anti-fog devices, warning signals, electric meters, lasers, metallurgical work;
- argon: incandescent, fluorescent, and "neon" lamps, metallurgical work, mercury thermometers, rectifier tubes, substitute for nitrogen in deep-sea diving systems, low temperature research, coolant in nuclear reactors, gas-liquid chromatography;
- krypton: "neon" and fluorescent lamps, lasers, high-speed photography;
- xenon: "neon," fluorescent, and high-intensity lamps, anesthetic (inhalation), diagnostic agent for blood flow and pulmonary function;
- radon: reaction initiator in scientific research, research on filtration properties, source of neutrons, testing of metal castings, cancer therapy.

5 What's in a name?

The following is information on household chemicals students might include in their charts.

Scientific: 2-amino-1,9-dihydro-9-[(2-hydroxyethoxy) methyl)]-6H-purin-6-one
Common: none
Generic: acyclovir
Brand: Aclovir, Vipral, Virorax, Zovirax

Scientific: sodium acetylsalicylic acid
Common: aspirin
Generic: aspirin
Brand: Alka Seltzer, Anacin, Bufferin, etc.

Scientific: ethyl *p*-aminobenzoate
Common: none
Generic: Benzocaine
Brand: Anbesol, Cetacaine, Chloraseptic, Therevac

Scientific: 7-chloro-1,3-dihydro-1-methlyl-5-phenyl-2H-1,4-benzodiazepin-2-one
Common: none
Generic: diazepam
Brand: (more than 20 brand names, the most common of which is Valium)

Scientific: 5-ethyl-5-phenyl-2,4,6(1H,3H,5H)-pyrim-idinetrione
Common: none
Generic: phenobarbital
Brand: Donnatal, Luminal, Quadrinal, etc.

Scientific: magnesium sulfate
Common: Epsom salts
Generic: none
Brand: Elder Caps, Vicon Forte

6 Photographic Development and Blueprints

Part One

Some compounds that might be mentioned include the following: Developers (B&W film): gallic acid, *o*-aminophenol, hydroquinone, *p*-methylaminophenol (metol), 1-phenyl-3-pyrazolidone (phenidone); Developers (color film): usually a substituted amine, such as N,N-diethyl-*p*-phenylethylenediamine; Stop bath: acetic acid, or some other weak acid; Fixer: sodium thiosulfate ("hypo").

Part Two

- Color film typically consists of four layers of color-sensitive emulsions placed on a supporting material. The top layer is sensitive to blue light. When blue light from a colored object strikes this layer, it reduces silver ions to form silver atoms. The blue layer is chosen as the top layer because silver halide ions are most sensitive to light in the blue region of the electromagnetic spectrum. Beneath the blue layer is a yellow filter. The yellow filter is used because it absorbs blue light (preventing it from penetrating further into the film) and transmits red and green (the combination of which produces yellow). Beneath the yellow filter are two more layers sensitive to green light and to red light. The color imparted to the blue, green, and red layers comes from cyanine dyes. These dyes make it possible for silver halide crystals in each of the layers to respond to a particular region of the electromagnetic spectrum. When this combination of layers is exposed to light, each responds to one of the three primary colors to produce the negative of the colored picture.
- The color of the positive produced from this negative results from cyan dyes formed during the developing process. The developer (usually a substituted amine) reacts with a coupler (such as a-naphthol) and silver ions to form a colored product. The pattern of colors formed in the final print then corresponds to the degree in which silver ions were not reduced in each of the colored layers during exposure of the film.

Conclusions

Student posters should include the following steps. Coating the paper: $Fe^{3+} + Fe(CN)_6^{3-} \rightarrow Fe[Fe(CN)_6]$ (green color) Photoreduction: $Fe^{3+} \rightarrow Fe^{2+}$; $3\ Fe^{2+} + Fe(CN)_6^{3-} \rightarrow Fe_3[Fe(CN)_6]_2$ (blue color)

7 Lighting the Dark

Activity

The majority of lamps that students will encounter are described in the Background Information to this activity. For additional information on these or other types of lamps refer to an encyclopedia or a reference on science and technology. The school librarian may be able to suggest special sources available to students at the school or in the community.

8 The Nitrogen Family: The Farmer's Best Friend

Survey

- In general, fertilizers are designated as direct if they contain one of the three main nutrient elements. Direct fertilizers are normally applied when a soil survey has revealed a deficiency in a particular element. Fertilizers that contain all three primary nutrients are known as mixed fertilizers.
- Inorganic pesticides are less popular today than they once were, but examples that might still be found include lead arsenate, sodium fluoride, borax, sulfur and lime sulfur, Bordeaux mixture, copper-chromium arsenic (CCA), and Paris green. Synthetic organic pesticides tend to fall into one of the following general categories: chlorinated hydrocarbons, organophosphates, carbonates, and synthetic pyrethroids.

Experiment

Students may not be able to find fertilizers that provide exact multiples of various nutrients, as suggested in the experiment directions. However, they should be able to find fertilizers that have more of one nutrient or another, while the other nutrients are kept constant. Using such materials, students should be able to develop a ratio between a given nutrient and the amount and/or rate of growth of their plants.

Report

- Student suggestions for the mini-unit will vary but should be sound from a content and a pedagogical point of view.
- Graphics will vary depending on the fertilizers and seeds chosen. The graphs should correctly represent the particular data.

9 Adhesives: Holding It All Together

Survey

Student surveys of adhesives and their uses and ingredients will vary. Some common examples of adhesives and their applications include the following: polyethylene and polypropylene (carpet backing); polyvinyl acetate (bookbinding and envelopes); polyvinyl chloride (pipe cement); epoxies (concrete adhesive); cyanoacrylates (in superglue); natural rubber and SBR [styrene-butadiene] (in masking tape); and starch glues (library paste).

Report

Student reports will vary, depending on the particular adhesives chosen.

10 Types of Glass

Activity

Ceramic glass: used for stove tops, laboratory bench tops, telescope mirrors; basic formula + TiO_2, or similar oxide.

Borosilicate glass: has a very low coefficient of expansion, not easily broken by sudden changes in temperature; used for most laboratory glassware; contains B_2O_3 and Al_2O_3.

Lead crystal glass: contains large amount of PbO; has a high refractive index, making it desirable for art objects.

Safety glass: in most common form, consists of two sheets of glass with a thin plastic sheet between them; used in automobile windows.

Photochromic glass: changes color when exposed to light; used in prescription glasses that change color in and out of the sunlight; contains a small amount of a photosensitive substance, such as a compound of gold, silver, or copper.

Window glass: very common form that contains about 72 percent SiO_2, 12 percent Na_2O, 10 percent CaO, 2 percent MgO, 1 percent Al_2O_3, and 3 percent K_2O.

Optical glass: used for camera and microscope lenses and other vision-adjusting devices; contains an excess of either PbO (flint glass) or CaO (crown glass).

Water glass: consists of sodium oxide and silicon dioxide only in a type of sodium silicate compound; has many industrial uses—as a catalyst, in sealing and laminating paper board containers, in water treatment plants, and in bleaching and sizing of textiles and paper pulp.

11 Artificial Atmospheres

Activity

Some features that students might mention for the artificial atmospheres given are as follows:

1. Scuba systems contain a regulator that allows air stored in a tank of compressed air to flow into the diver's mouthpiece. Exhaled air is expelled through an outlet valve to the water.
2. Nineteenth-century diving bells used ordinary air under pressure greater than atmospheric pressure.
3. Deep-sea diving suits are filled with air supplied through a long hose from a compressor on a boat on the water's surface.
4. A fluorescent lamp contains mercury vapor. When the lamp is turned on, an electrical current flows through the vapor, causing it to emit ultraviolet light that, in turn, causes a phosphor on the inside of the tube to glow.

5. A sodium-vapor lamp contains sodium vapor which, when energized by an electric current, emits a yellow glow.
6. Early United States spacecraft used pure oxygen atmospheres, a factor in the 1967 deaths of three astronauts. Soviet and current U.S. spacecraft use oxygen diluted with an inert gas, such as nitrogen.
7. Commercial aircraft circulate an atmosphere of normal atmospheric composition at high speed (10,000 cubic feet per minute in a Boeing 747).
8. The atmospheres used to protect important documents consist of helium, argon, or another inert gas that prevents the documents from damage of oxidation.
9. Metals being treated at high temperatures are prevented from oxidizing or undergoing other chemical changes by being covered with a blanket of an inert gas, such as argon or helium.
10. "Clean rooms" are filled with ordinary air at a pressure greater than normal atmospheric pressure to prevent dust and other forms of contamination from entering the room when doors are opened.

12 Making STPP: Sodium Tripolyphosphate

Suggest that students refer to college chemistry textbooks or specialized books on industrial chemistry for additional information.

13 A Hard Day at the Laundromat

Experiment

- The softened water will require fewer drops of soap.
- Student scales of water hardness will vary.
- Results of the liquid-soap test will vary depending on the water samples chosen.

Report

Student speeches will vary, but should correctly reflect the information on water softness.

14 Adding Spice to Your Daily Diet: Acidulants as Food Additives

Research

- Solution A is 0.5%; Solution B is 0.05%; Solution C is 0.005%
- The sensitivity of various individuals to acid tastes will vary from person to person. Some individuals may not detect an acid taste at all in Solution C, or even in Solution B. In most cases, however, tasters will be able to detect an increasing amount of acidity in going from Solution C to Solution B to Solution A.
- You may want to point out to students or have them test for a "fatigue" factor, which is that one's ability to detect any flavor, such as acidity, is affected by previous exposure to that flavor. The more trials a taster has had in this experience, the less well he or she will be able to distinguish an acid taste in later trials.

15 pH in the pHlower Garden

- The results of Experiments 1 and 2 will vary according to the soil samples tested.
- Students will observe that the more acidic the soil, the more lime solution is needed to neutralize the soil.

16 What a Rotten Apple: Food Preservation Techniques

Part One

See chart below.

Chemical	Mechanism	Uses/Foods Used In
Salt (NaCl)	antibacterial; absorbs water	salting; curing; drying meats
$NaNO_2$	prevents growth of *C. botulinum* bacteria	meat products
Sorbic acid	prevents growth of molds and fungi	cheeses, mayonnaise, jellies, syrups, cakes, soft drinks, etc.
Citric acid	binds to metal ions to prevent oxidation	ice creams and sherbets, fruit drinks, jellies, canned fruits and vegetables, etc.
Ascorbic acid	preferentially oxidized before foods	beverages, breakfast foods, dried potatoes
BHA and BHT	preferentially oxidized before foods	oils and shortenings, potato chips, candy, chewing gum, etc.
Propyl gallate	preferentially oxidized before foods	fats and oils, meat products, soups, chewing gum

Part Two

Fresh-squeezed apple juice can be purchased in many grocery stores.

Report

1. As evidence of spoilage, students may mention foaming of the apple juice, cloudiness of the juice, or the formation of mold on the surface of the juice.
2. Since the concentration of citric acid solutions varies in the sequence A>B>C>D>E, the rate of spoilage of the apple juice should vary in the sequence A<B<C<D<E. The apple juice with the least concentrated citric acid solution will likely take about a week to show signs of spoilage.
3. Students should discover that the less concentrated the citric acid solution, the less time it takes for apple juice to spoil.

17 What's New in Batteries

Exercise

Some battery types students might find are nickelcadmium, silver cell, mercury cell, alkaline cell, lithium, and zinc-nickel oxide batteries. The composition of some types varies, of course. The detailed information students need to sketch battery structure and discuss their operation can be found in college-level chemistry texts and a few application-oriented high school chemistry texts.

18 A More Beautiful You ... Thanks to Chemistry

Experiment 1

To prepare a water bath, half-fill a large beaker with water. Place a smaller beaker containing the beeswax (available at beauty and natural food stores) and mineral oil in the water-filled beaker. Gently heat the water with a Bunsen burner or hot plate. Stir the water from time to time, being careful not to splash any water into the beeswax-oil mixture. Maintain the desired temperature by continuing to apply heat as needed.

Experiment 2

- To prepare agar solution, add 2.5 g of dehydrated nutrient agar to 100 mL of distilled water. Heat until dissolved.
- Air can contain pathogenic bacteria that might land on the agar and grow. Therefore, when bacteria are cultured in class, take every precaution to avoid contamination with pathogenic forms. Once the agar has been exposed to the air for the initial 15 minutes, be sure that the lids remain on the dishes. You might have students tape the lids to the bottoms to avoid accidents. Dispose of the petri dishes and their contents in accordance with local regulations when the activity is completed.

19 Cooking Chemistry

Activity 1

- Student results will vary. However, in general, custard that is cooked too quickly will burn easily. Cooking custard too long or using too high a temperature will break the custard into curds, giving it a "scrambled-egg" appearance. The effect of added ingredients will vary depending on the type.
- A general formula for making custard is 1 egg plus 2 egg yolks per cup of liquid. For liquid, you can use milk, cream, water, juices, broths, or any combination of these items.

Activity 2

You may wish to have a selection of cookbooks available in the classroom from which students can obtain recipes for making crème anglaise and crème patissière. The preparation of each dish requires some modest culinary skill, so the final products produced by various students may differ from each other even if the methods of preparation are the same. Examples of each dish may be compared with each other to determine whether differences among them reflect chemical changes or differences in the cook's skills.

20 Energy from Solid Wastes

Report

Student reports will vary, but should include both pro and con arguments. Pro arguments include the need for waste disposal and for energy production. Con arguments emphasize pollution caused by greenhouse gases, transport traffic, and aesthetics.

21 Medical Uses of Radioisotopes

Exercise

Some uses of specific radioisotopes are listed in the table below.

Radioisotope	Uses
Chromium-54	studies of red blood cells
Gallium-67	studies of tumors and abscesses
Iodine-131	thyroid studies
Phosphorus-32	skin cancer studies
Sodium-24	studies of circulatory system
Thallium-201	heart studies